SCHIRMER'S LIBRARY
OF MUSICAL CLASSICS

Vol. 1894

ANTONIO VIVALDI

Six Sonatas

For Double Bass and Piano

Realized by
NIKOLAI GRAUDAN

Solo Part Edited by
LUCAS DREW

G. SCHIRMER, *Inc.*

DISTRIBUTED BY
HAL•LEONARD®
CORPORATION
7777 W. BLUEMOUND RD. P.O. BOX 13819 MILWAUKEE, WI 53213

PREFACE

The editor is indebted to Nikolai Graudan for his musical and scholarly realization and editing of the *Six Sonatas for Violoncello and Continuo* by Antonio Vivaldi. The following is part of the preface to Mr. Graudan's edition for cello:

"The original manuscript of the *Six Sonatas á Violoncello solo* by Antonio Vivaldi (in the Bibliothèque Nationale of Paris) consists of 42 pages on which the cello part and the bass (not figured) are written very neatly and plainly on two staves. There are but a few instances in the musical notation which might be considered slips of the pen. In contrast, many of the bowings are inaccurate and approximate.

"In order to present a true picture of Vivaldi's manuscript the cello part of the piano score has been left un-edited, except for the inevitable adjustment of the position of the slurs. The bass is original, but it has sometimes been moved an octave lower or doubled. The few corrections in the text are clearly indicated."

The following additions are found in this performance edition for double bass:

1. *Tempo* definitions have been made more specific, and some descriptive terms have been added.

2. *Dynamic* markings have been provided.

3. Additional *bowings* have been indicated.

4. Possible fingerings (Roman numerals represent strings — i.e. I, "G" string; II, "D" string, etc.).

5. Notes with dots under a slur ⌢ are short, those with dashes ⌢ are long with but a slight separation.

6. ⌢ denotes a clear separation between the notes with the bow resuming its movement in the same direction.

7. Where two different bowings are marked in the last bar of a movement, the upper is to be used before the repeat, the lower for the ending.

8. Ornaments are clearly indicated. Some have been rhythmically notated.

The following is an example of the original manuscript (Largo-Sonata No. 3):

It is hoped that the *Sonatas,* presented in this edition as a musical unit, will be useful to double bassists.

Lucas Drew

Sonata No. 1

Realized by Nikolai Graudan

Antonio Vivaldi
(1678 - 1741)

Largo (ma non troppo)

Violoncello

Piano

Allegro

Largo (maestoso)

Allegro (gaio)

Sonata No. 2

Allegro (deciso)

1) MS 2) MS 3) MS

14

Largo (non troppo, amoroso)

Allegro (con brio)

* MS

Sonata No. 3

Largo

Allegro (energico)

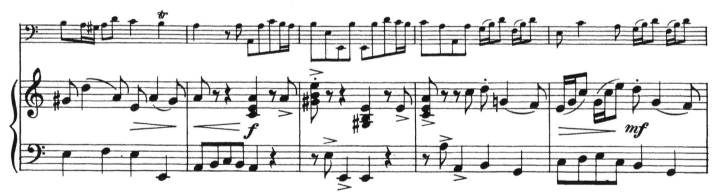

Largo

Allegro (Allegretto moderato, poco giocondo)

Double Bass

SCHIRMER'S LIBRARY
OF MUSICAL CLASSICS

Vol. 1894

Antonio Vivaldi

Six Sonatas
For Double Bass and Piano

Solo Part Edited by
LUCAS DREW

G. SCHIRMER, Inc.

DISTRIBUTED BY

HAL•LEONARD®
CORPORATION
7777 W. BLUEMOUND RD. P.O. BOX 13819 MILWAUKEE, WI 53213

Sonata No. 1

Double Bass

Solo part edited
by Lucas Drew

Antonio Vivaldi
(1678-1741)

Double Bass

Double Bass

Largo (maestoso)

Double Bass

Allegro (gaio)

Sonata No. 2

Double Bass

Largo (non troppo, amoroso)

Double Bass

Allegro (con brio)

Double Bass
Sonata No.3

Double Bass

Double Bass

Double Bass

Double Bass

Sonata No.4

Double Bass

Double Bass

Largo (mesto)

Allegro (quasi Allegretto)

Double Bass

Double Bass
Sonata No.5

Double Bass

Double Bass

Double Bass
Sonata No.6

Largo

Allegro(non troppo)

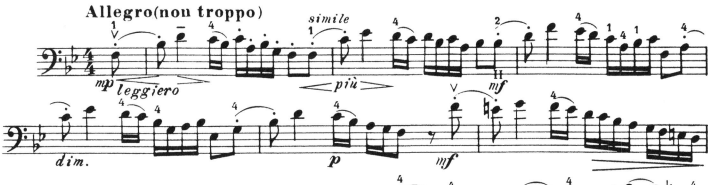

Double Bass

Double Bass

Sonata No. 4

Allegro (vivace)

Largo (mesto)

Allegro (quasi Allegretto)

Sonata No. 5

Allegro (ma non troppo)

Largo (doloroso)

Allegro (con spirito)

Sonata No. 6

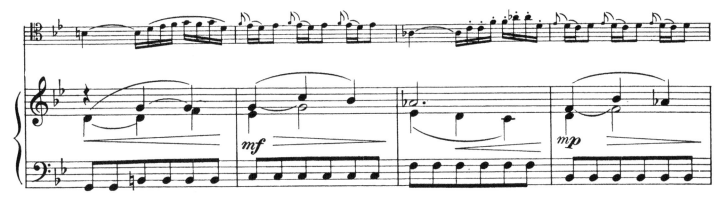

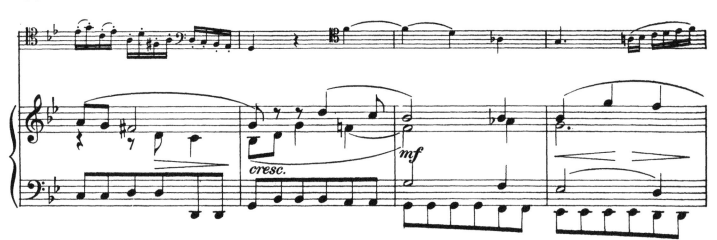

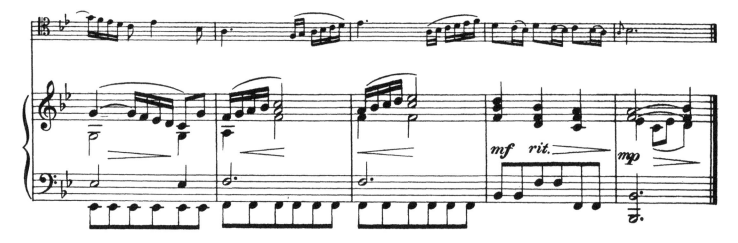

Allegro (non troppo)

Largo (doloroso)

*MS

Allegro (spiritoso)